MW00440920

Rugby Basics: Your Beginners Guide

ISBN-13: 978-1479261482

ISBN-10: 1479261483

Copyright Notice

All Rights Reserved © 2012 Dave Rantree

RUGBY BASICS: YOUR BEGINNERS GUIDE

Dave Rantree

I dedicate this book to every person – who has been lucky enough to have their lives touched by the joy, excitement and sheer buzz of rugby...

Contents

The History of Rugby

Rugby is one game that many people all over the world may be fairly familiar with. If you're interested in learning this sport, then it's best for you to familiarise its history and rules first.

Take note that this is an extremely tough sport and attempting to play it without knowing much about its background or its rules could have you ending up in the emergency room of the nearest hospital.

In fact, there have been instances when people actually died as a result of playing this sport without knowing the rules or taking the necessary precautions. Naturally, you'll want to make sure that doesn't happen to you.

The tough sport of rugby has quite a long history. There are some scholars who hold the belief that the game traces its origins back to the ancient Romans.

However, the most popular belief is that it actually began in the year 1823 when football player William Webb Ellis ran holding the football in his arms rather than kicking it with his feet.

This theory owes its popularity to the fact that it coincides with another theory, which states that sometime between 1820 and 1830, football players were allowed to run with the ball.

A powerful football player named Jem Mackie then helped make this way of playing the game permanent in the period between 1838 and 1839. But, it only became a legal type of play in the 1841 to 1842 season.

Due to the high level of risk and danger the game involved, official rules were finally established in 1845.

With the establishment of these rules, the game also officially became an entirely separate game from football. The established rules governed how rugby was played for fifteen years, with the exception of one amendment in 1848.

This was the year when the Cambridge Rules, which has to do with the players' use of their hands and the football, were established.

In 1863, another amendment was made to the rules as a ban on tripping and hacking was implemented.

The ban also included a prohibition on the act of holding the ball in a player's hands and then running with it towards the goal after it has been caught. These days, though, the rules of the game are pretty much like the Cambridge Rules.

The original rugby ball was made from the bladder of a pig, which needed to be blown up before a game.

And because the bladder used was usually freshly taken from a pig, nobody really wanted to be responsible for the task of blowing up the ball.

These days, rugby balls are hand-sewn, weigh about 12 to 13 ounces, and usually have a length of 11 to 11.25 inches. The circumference of the ball being used these days has to be 30 to 31 inches at its largest part and it should have a width of 25.5 to 26 inches.

Furthermore, the ball should have no more than eight stitches for every inch of its length.

If you're serious about getting into the sport of rugby, then you need to be extra cautious about protecting yourself from possible injuries.

Although regulation rugby uniforms don't include helmets, any player would be smart to use one.

It's also advisable for you to use elbow guards, knee pads, shin guards, and a chest plate. You should always bear in mind that rugby can be a very rough sport.

And before you even start training to become a rugby player, it would be wise for you to spend some time watching a few games so you'll have a clearer idea as to how it is played.

When you finally go out on the field for your first rugby game, you should also observe how the play is coming along, as it can change quite abruptly and a player who's not observant or alert enough has an increased chance of getting injured.

An Overview of Rugby

The game of rugby is very popular in places like England, New Zealand, and Australia. These days, it is already being played in other countries as well.

The sport was officially created sometime in the nineteenth century, but was only truly able to gain popularity in August of 1985. The sport traces its origins to the sport of football, but soon moved away from it when a different set of rules was developed especially for rugby.

If you're interested in learning to play this game, then you'll need to familiarise it and learn as much as you can about it before you even begin training to become a rugby player. The following overview should get you off to a good start.

Rules of the Game

The main difference between football and rugby has to do with the ball and the manner in which it is handled.

Football players kick a round-shaped ball across the field whereas rugby players use an oval-shaped ball that can either be kicked or carried across the playing field.

Two points are awarded to the team for every goal that's made in rugby, as opposed to football, which awards a single point for every goal made. A rugby game lasts for eighty minutes, with each team given six tackles or downs in every play.

Rugby Tournaments

The most awaited rugby tournament is the Rugby League World Cup. Other than this, the Four Nations Cup is also quite popular with rugby enthusiasts. In fact, it is during the Four Nations tournament that the betting fever is most strongly felt in the world of rugby.

Another big rugby tournament is the Challenge Cup, which involves the four major rugby teams. It can be a bit difficult to point out which among these four teams is the best, especially since there have been lots of times when the Challenge Cup was actually awarded to none of the teams.

During these instances, only the Man of the Match award and the Lance Todd Trophy were given out.

The former is chosen by league reporters whereas the latter was awarded to the player who is adjudged as the show stealer in the tournament.

Another big rugby game is the Super League, which is basically a European tournament, but mostly played by teams from the United Kingdom.

Betting in Rugby

It is very rare for a tie to occur in a rugby match, which makes rugby betting so much easier than football betting. Bookies in this case usually set handicaps according to the difference in the points.

These days, it has also become quite common for people to join online betting, particularly after the Championship of Six Nations in Europe and the Tri Nations.

Online betting in rugby was never a popular activity in the past. But, with the increase in the popularity of the sport, the betting activities have also been enhanced.

In sum, you need to bear in mind that rugby is a tough and dangerous game.

The element of danger is what makes it very exciting to watch. It is also what attracts many people to actually playing the game.

Finally, it is the very reason why you need to take the necessary precautions before getting engaged in the sport.

Rugby Gear and Equipment

Just like any other sport, rugby requires players to use a number of specialized equipment in order to facilitate a successful and fair encounter between the two teams on the playing field.

A tough, rough, and largely physical game, you can expect to experience more than a few blows and tugs when you play a match.

The good news is that there are a number of manufacturers that offer a wide range of rugby gear that can help you avoid injuries and add to your enjoyment of the game.

With a wide range of choices, you'll surely be able to find the right gear to suit your purposes.

Headgear for rugby players is typically made from a light synthetic material that has the ability to protect you from any strong impact.

One thing you need to make sure of is that the headgear you use has the approval of the International Rugby Board.

Another important piece of gear you should use as a rugby player is a gum shield, which not only provides your teeth and gums with the necessary protection, but also helps reduce the damage or injury you may suffer along your jaw line.

Gum shields are typically moulded specifically to fit your teeth and gums.

You should also buy a rugby kit, which is typically comprised of a pair of rugby shorts, rugby boots, and some rugby shirts. Some kits included a few accessories, but these three are the main components of a rugby kit.

Rugby shorts are usually made of cotton and feature pockets, reinforced seams, tie cords, and elastic waistbands.

There are also fusion shorts without pockets that are available and produced specifically to match fusion shirts.

Rugby shirts, which are typically known as rugby jerseys, are generally knitted with precision so it can withstand the pulling and tugging players commonly encounter on the rugby field.

Rugby shirts are also necessarily lightweight and strong while still being comfortable to use so it doesn't take anything away from a player's speed and overall performance.

They're typically made of a combination of cotton and polyester as well as acrylic fabric.

Rugby boots typically have studded soles and the studs can be made of either plastic or a dull metal. These studs enable players to move with adequate grip on the playing field. Before you shop for a pair of rugby boots, make sure you perfectly understand the size and shape of your feet.

Another thing you need to understand is your personal style of running, which can also affect the level of comfort you experience when moving on the field with your boots on.

Another important consideration when choosing rugby gear is protection for you upper body.

Just like when choosing rugby shirts, light weight, strength, and comfort are the three most important factors you need to consider when choosing upper body protection.

Of course, you shouldn't neglect perfect fit while you're at it. Take note that the areas of your upper body that are most vulnerable to injury in a rugby game are your shoulders and chest area. Finally, you'll need a rugby ball of good quality.

The latest technology has offered a lot of improvements in the hand-stitched leather rugby ball. It is now waterproof and much easier to handle even in slippery conditions.

Remember to always consider the quality of a product when you shop for any of the rugby gear and equipment mentioned above.

Rugby Positions

In learning how to play rugby, you'll have to familiarise the different rugby positions.

Each position in a rugby team lets the player know where he should stand on the playing field, what their individual duties are as a player, and how they fit into the entire play of the team.

There are a total of 15 rugby positions for each team, but these positions have gone through several changes over the years. In fact, the names of the positions may even vary from one country to another, thus making the topic a bit confusing for people who aren't very familiar with the game.

In Australia and New Zealand, for example, players who hold positions as backs are named according to the distance they stand from the scrum.

Back positions in these two countries are therefore known as halves, centres, five-eighths, three-quarters, and full backs.

In other countries, particularly those in the Northern Hemisphere, the half back position is typically known as the scrum half position, the five-eighths is called the fly half, and the centres are known as either the inside or outside centre.

As regards the forwards positions in rugby, players standing in the first two rows of the scrum are typically known as the tight five.

They're usually the ones who do most of the hard work in a match. They generally win the ball in such close situations as scrums, line outs, and rucks.

Players standing on the third row of the scrum are generally known as flankers. They're positioned on each side of the row and the number eight stands between them.

The three players on this row are also collectively known as the loose forwards. They're also casually called the loosies.

The two players positioned on the outside of the front row are typically known as the props.

The reason for this name is that they're mostly responsible for propping up between them the hooker who tries to hook the rugby ball back to his teammates whenever it is played into the scrum.

The props are typically among the strongest players, since they're not only responsible for supporting the hooker, but also for lifting other players at the line out so as to assist them in reaching for the ball.

A rugby team's props are traditionally numbered one and three, and they'd have to stand at their positions in the line out to support their team's main jumpers. A team will always have at least two jumpers in an effort to confuse the opposing team.

Other than trying to hook the rugby ball in the scrum, the team's hooker is also responsible for throwing the rugby ball in for the line outs.

The second row of the scrum consists of the two tallest players in a rugby team. These players are known as the locks and they're responsible for holding the scrum together and for providing the team's main forward thrust so as to push the opposing team off of the ball.

They're also often the team's main jumpers in the line out primarily due to their height. These days, however, the world of rugby is seeing more and more of the other players getting involved in the line outs.

Rules of the Game

Learning the rules of the game is necessarily among the first steps you take in your effort to learn how to play the game and perhaps someday become one of the world's best rugby players.

Simply put, rugby is a team game that involves the main objective of scoring more points than the opposing team.

There are two general ways in which you can score a point.

The first is by getting a try and the second is by kicking the rugby ball over the crossbar to score a penalty. Scoring a try means your team is awarded five points plus the option to try for an additional two points by kicking the ball between the posts over the crossbar.

This additional kick is known as a conversion and it allows you to score a maximum of seven points from a single try.

Try refers to the act of touching the ball to the ground over the opposing team's goal line.

Each team in a rugby match is required to position 15 players on the field.

They're also allowed to have a maximum of seven players each on the bench. These players may be substituted onto the playing field during the match. A rugby match lasts for eighty minutes and is subdivided into two 40-minute halves.

There are generally two basic positions in a rugby game, and these are the forwards and the backs.

Players holding the forwards positions are generally bigger and stronger whereas those who hold the back positions are typically smaller and faster, since it's their responsibility to run with the ball as soon as the forwards pass it on to them.

Rugby players holding forwards positions are further subdivided into the front row with three players, the second row with two players, and the back row with three players.

Each of these groups relate to the position of the players in the scrum, which is comprised of three rows of players.

Two players holding back positions are known as the halves, four players are known as the three-quarters, and one player is known as the fullback.

Although there are a lot of rules in the sport of rugby, the basic rules can be understood quire easily. The rugby has to be passed backwards at all times, but players are allowed to kick it forwards.

Any of the players on the field can run with the ball, but a player who is tackled to the ground has to release the ball to give the opposing team a chance to pick it up.

You need to remember as well that rugby players are only allowed to touch the ball when they're on their feet, which is why they need to release it as soon as they're tackled to the ground.

Whenever the rugby ball goes off the pitch on either side, a line out is called. This line out is similar to the throw-in in the game of soccer.

A player from the opposing team will then throw the rugby ball back into play and then a number of the remaining players on the field will line up in order to receive the ball.

The exact number of receivers may vary, depending on the discretion of the throwing team.

Whenever the ball goes off the pitch on either end, it is then kicked back into play from the line situated 22 metres from the goal line. Now, you should be ready to start training for rugby.

Getting Into Shape

As you probably know by now, rugby is a very tough sport. Those who choose to play this game shouldn't be afraid of getting knocked about, of risking injury, and of taking a hit in an effort to achieve victory.

More than that, though, you'll have to be able to keep up with the speed and power of your team's plays, overwhelm the players of the opposing team, and last for the entire game in order to be deemed a good rugby player.

So, how can you achieve the necessary level of speed, power, and strength?

What kind of training routine can help prepare you for the task of dominating your next rugby match?

Following is a discussion on the components of an effective training regimen that'll surely have you dominating the rugby playing field when game time comes.

The very first thing you need to focus on is endurance.

After all, your speed and power will hardly do you any good if you can't last for more than a few minutes on the field.

You'll have to be able to maintain your speed for extended periods of time while the game is going on.

You also have to develop the ability to cross the field several times successively without losing steam.

Towards this end, it's advisable for you to engage in a good combination of short and long distance running performed in intervals.

This means you need to run for longer distances once or twice each week and make sure you can pass the speaking test while doing so. You should also engage in interval training twice each week.

Interval training works by giving you the opportunity to test and push your body. It involves doing bouts of high intensity exercises for shorter durations and with minimal breaks in between exercises.

When training for rugby, this could mean running as fast as you can for eight minutes, taking a three-minute break, and then running for another eight minutes.

It's best to do three sets of these eight-minute runs. This type of interval training also works for sprints as long as you vary the combinations and distances in order to develop a good variety of endurance and speed. Variety is, in fact, one of the key elements of getting into shape for the sport of rugby.

The next thing you need to work on is your strength. This means you'll have to hit the gym.

When you do, be careful not to waste any of your time on isolation machines or any of those fancy fitness toys. What you need to do instead is grab a barbell and start doing some serious work.

The strength training exercises you perform at the gym should be ones that involve such basic compound moves as deadlifts, squats, bench presses, shoulders presses, clean and jerks, and pull-ups.

Remember to focus on developing your strength, power, explosive speed, and form. You'll surely thank yourself for doing so once you start seeing the results of your training on the rugby field.

Preventing Injuries

Injuries are practically inevitable in any sport, from bruises to shin splints to torn ligaments to fractured bones. This is especially true of a sport as rough and tough as rugby.

As a rugby player, therefore, one of your primary goals should be to keep yourself protected from these possible injuries. In fact, you should learn how to avoid injury before you even step onto a rugby field for your first game.

The good news for you is that most sports have a corresponding protective gear designed to keep you safe. Baseball players have their cups, football players have their pads, and soccer players have their shin guards.

For rugby players, there's also an entire set of protective gear that can shield you when you get tackled and repeatedly hit in the course of a game.

You may be tough enough to take a hit or two, but you should remember that being tough isn't enough to prevent injury when you're playing rugby.

This is one sport that involves a lot of collisions and bruises, cuts, strains, and concussions are likely to occur unless you're adequately protected.

The key to protecting yourself from injury in rugby is proper training. It is important for you to always use proper technique whether you're practicing or in an actual game.

It may not really be much fun to keep practicing the fundamentals, but making sure you tackle, scrum, and ruck properly is crucial to ensuring your safety.

You need to constantly develop your basic skills and make sure you know your position all throughout the game. A rugby player needs to know his abilities and limitations in order to play this game safely.

For example, if you play the position of a prop, then you should never stand on the wing in the back line. It's highly important for you to learn the rules of the game by heart before you even start playing.

Aside from using proper technique, knowing your position and the rules of the game, you should also keep your body fit in order to prevent injury in rugby.

In fact, strength training, speed training, and skills training are highly valuable to rugby players.

Among other things, you should always remember to stretch and warm up properly before starting a training session.

Furthermore, you should always make sure that you eat right because proper nutrition can also be very helpful for keeping your body fit.

In case you do suffer from any form of injury, be careful not to add any stress on it.

You should instead take a break and focus on improving your performance in other aspects of the game.

It's also a good idea to use scrum machines and tackling pads during training so as to avoid hurting yourself or a teammate.

For players in the forwards positions, the ability to scrum is among the key aspects of a good game and a scrum machine allows you to practice without possibly injuring anyone.

A tackling pad, for its part, can help both forwards and backs learn proper technique. Bear in mind that it's very important for you to wrap up when you tackle.

By following the above guidelines and wearing protective gear, you'll surely enjoy rugby even more, as you can play with more assurance of your safety.

Proper Nutrition

If you truly want to perform well as a rugby player, then you shouldn't just focus on learning the necessary skills for the game.

You should also gain at least a basic understanding of what the proper nutrition for an athlete is.

It's important that you find just the right balance of carbohydrates, protein, and fats in order for your body to have enough fuel to sustain you in a rugby game as well as in the training you'll be engaged in.

Your body has the capacity to survive even the toughest of competitions and the most rigorous training activities, but only if you supply it with the right kinds of food in just the right amounts for it to stay healthy, strong, and energized.

Let us first take a look at carbohydrates. Contrary to what you may often hear in the news or read in articles about dieting, carbohydrates are not the bad guys in nutrition.

In fact, they're an important part of your regular diet because they're generally responsible for increasing your energy levels.

As an athlete, increased energy may be exactly what you need to be able to push your body to its limits without risking your safety or your health. The best sources of carbohydrates are rice, potatoes, bread, and pasta.

Take note that 60% of your regular diet has to be comprised of carbohydrates, since you're putting your body through a considerable amount of physical activity as an athlete.

Another important component of an athlete's diet is protein, which makes up your body's building blocks. If you've been working out for some time, then you probably already know that protein is crucial to muscle building.

As a rugby player, you also know that muscle building is crucial to an excellent performance on the playing field.

It is recommended that protein should make up 20% of your regular diet, the best sources of which are meats, fish, beans, legumes, quinoa, and cheese.

You may also want to consider drinking protein shakes or taking protein supplements to boost your protein levels.

Fat is also another component that has always been cast as the bad guy, where dieting is concerned. The truth is that a healthy diet necessarily includes a certain amount of fat. What's bad for you isn't fat per se, but too much fat and the wrong kinds of fat.

Remember, though, that taking in too little fat is just as bad as taking in too much.

Fat is necessary because it helps build up your cells and hormone levels while also giving you a healthy energy reserve.

While you do need to keep your fat levels low, you should make sure they don't go lower than 20% of your regular diet.

The best sources of the right kinds of fat for a healthy diet are dairy products, avocadoes, nuts, and olive oil.

Of course, you shouldn't neglect your liquid intake as well.

It's best to drink about two litres of water each day to flush out any toxins from your body and effectively distribute the nutrients you get from your food to the different parts of your body.

Remember to keep your fluid intake up before and during a game.

More importantly, always remember to replace the fluids you've lost in the game by drinking water as soon as the game ends. For a more personalised nutrition plan, it's best for you to visit your local nutritionist.

Finding a Good Coach

Sure, you can learn all about the rules of rugby simply by reading a few articles online. You may even learn the fundamentals of the game by watching a few videos.

But, because rugby is a highly physical and considerably dangerous sport, it becomes highly essential for you to find a good coach.

There are a number of important qualities you need to look for in a rugby coach. As an aspiring rugby player, it is indeed in your best interest to become aware of these qualities before you join a rugby team.

As a sport, rugby requires strength, agility, and a high level of athleticism. A good rugby coach is one who can take these raw attributes and hone them so as to create a team the world will surely notice.

The most basic quality you should look for in a rugby coach is a thorough and deep understanding of the game. A good coach is one who knows more than just the rules of the game.

He should also have a clear understanding of how each player can be used in the game to make things work to your team's advantage.

Furthermore, a good coach should have the ability to create specific plays and use the best talents of each player.

Another skill a rugby coach should possess, which takes some time to develop, is the ability to make the right decisions quickly during a game.

For example, he may be placed in a position where he needs to decide whether to switch players or wait a few minutes more before making the switch.

A few minutes can have a huge impact in the results of the game, which is why a coach has to be able to decide very quickly.

Respect for players and the ability to build positive relationships is another important quality for a rugby coach to have.

If a coach is unable to build a connection or a good relationship with his players, then it can be difficult for him to establish his leadership and earn his players' respect.

Consequently, it will be almost impossible to expect positive results from his players. A coach needs to create an atmosphere of mutual respect without actually resorting to becoming friends with his players. This allows him to make unbiased decisions during a game, based purely on talent and skill.

Finally, a good rugby coach is one who has vision. This is a team's ticket towards winning the game. The coach you choose should have the ability to look at his players and quickly learn how to play towards his team's strengths while preying on the opposing team's weaknesses.

The ability to create excellent plays, teach rugby skills, create optimal lines, and use break downs are all just parts of the overall vision of a good coach.

As an aspiring rugby player, you should know that for the most part, you can only be as good as your coach will allow you to be.

Therefore, if you want to become the best player you can possibly be, then you have to make sure you find the right coach and join the right team.

Rugby can be a lot of fun and a very rewarding sport as long as you take the necessary steps to learn it in the best way possible.

Speed Training

Speed and agility are two of the most valuable assets of any rugby player. Therefore, if you really want to become an excellent rugby player, you'll have to work on improving your speed even as a beginner.

Here are some drills that may help make you quicker on your feet:

1. Ankle Weights Drill

As a beginner, it's advisable for you to try completing five full-length sprints on the pitch every other day with weights attached to your ankles.

For your first two sprints, you may want to go at 60% of your maximum pace and then increase that to 75% on the third sprint, 85% on the fourth sprint and then at full pace on the fifth sprint.

As regards the weights, you may want to start off with 2.5 lbs. and then increase it gradually as you advance. As a rest period between sprints, walk or jog back to the starting line. When you finally run without ankle weights, you'll notice that you feel a lot lighter and fitter.

2. Weighted Vest Drill

To execute this drill, you'll have to do full length sprints every other day while wearing a weighted vest.

It's best for you to start off with a weight of five kilograms for the first week and then increase it to seven kilograms on the second week and then ten kilograms on the third week.

Just as with the first drill, you should walk or jog back to the starting line so you'll have a rest period between sprints. Since this drill is quite strenuous, it may be wise to consult with your doctor first and make sure you're in a good enough shape for this.

3. Parachute Drill

This drill is done by sprinting with a parachute backpack. This is a lighter version of the previous drill and is, in fact, the perfect cool down drill after doing a round of weighted vest sprints.

You may also use this drill on its own as some sort of practice a couple of weeks before you start doing the weighted vest drill.

It's best to do five sprints with the usual walk in between sprints and then slowly jog around the pitch before doing another five sprints. Just like the two other drills, you can get the best results by doing this drill every other day.

Whatever type of drill you decide to work on, you should always remember to warm up beforehand and cool down afterwards in order to prevent injury and to maximise the benefits of the drill.

The good thing about these drills is that they enhance not only your speed, but also your mental ability, fitness level, and confidence, which are all important attributes of a good rugby player.

Pretty soon, you should find yourself zooming way ahead of your opponents as you learn to move faster than ever and start to feel so much lighter on your feet.

Such amazing speed, when coupled with well-enhanced skills, should make you a player to be feared on the field.

Strength Training

Regardless of their position, rugby players need to have high strength and endurance levels as a foundation for their fitness.

If you want to build a career in this sport, therefore, you'll have to organize your strength and power training during the off-season to get yourself ready for the next rugby season.

Remember that high muscle mass is a prerequisite for doing well in this tough sport and a well-organized strength training program will surely help you development the most important muscles for excellent performance.

Among the things you need to take note of is the importance of the relationship between monotony and recovery.

Bear in mind that a monotonous training typically doesn't give room for recovery. That's because monotonous programs usually require you to train on consecutive days at the same intensity levels.

You should give room for recovery by mixing it up and assigning days of high intensity training as well as days for low intensity workouts.

Low intensity days may involve doing aerobics or circuits.

You should also remember to assign at least one day each week for rest.
One of the best ways to organize your strength training program is to break it down into phases with a specific objective that'll eventually lead to the achievement of your overall goal.

For example, you may want to follow a general fitness program for the first two to three weeks with the objective of preparing your muscles and tendons for the more intense workouts in the next phases.

During this phase, it's best to use weight machines and set the intensity at 50-60% of the maximum you can lift.

Stretching and flexibility work is also necessary at this time as well as conditioning of your core muscles and neck. Aerobic and anaerobic conditioning should also be achieved in this phase.

After the general fitness phase, you may want to start a hypertrophy phase, which aims to develop your muscle cross-section.

The muscles to be developed during this phase are responsible for your power, sprinting speed, effective tackling, and accurate passing.
The next phase is called the maximum strength phase, as it aims to finally develop your strength.

The main objective of this phase is to train your nervous system to recruit your newly-built muscles.

This period should last for three to eight weeks and use an intensity of 80-95% of the maximum you can lift. This phase should see you developing considerable amounts of muscle tension.

The next phase is known as the power phase and it involves resistance work that should be done at an intensity range of 30-90%.

During this phase, you should allow for both intra-rest and inter-rest recovery. Intra-rest refers to the period of rest in between repetitions while inter-rest refers to the period of rest in between sets.

Finally, you need to go through a maintenance phase, which aims to maintain the strength you've gained from your exercises all throughout the season.

Therefore, this phase will most likely occur during the season itself. By properly organizing your off-season strength training program, you'll surely be able to look forward to a great rugby season!

Performing a Tackle

Since you've taken interest in playing rugby, then you probably want to learn how to execute a good tackle.

Before you start doing so, take note that the tackle involves the highest amount of risk for injury in this sport. This is why it's very important for you to do it just right.

Here are some of the most important points you need to bear in mind when you execute a front-on tackle in rugby:

- ✗ Never cross your feet.

- ✗ Never drop your chin during a tackle, as that can cause concussions and neck injury.

- ✓ Always follow the attacking player and then run towards his shoulder that's farthest from the touchline.

- ✓ Stay square to the attacker as long as you can in order to deny him space.

- ✓ Keep your eyes open and be sure to check where you're going to make contact with the attacker.

- ✓ Remember that footwork can be deceiving, so you should focus instead on the area between the attacking player's hips and chest.

- ✓ Place emphasis on your back position to make sure you have a stronger, lower, and more powerful tackle.

- ✓ Align your head to either side of the attacking player rather than the front of his body and avoid making contact using the top of your head.

- ✓ Follow the hit's direction with your head.

- ✓ Be sure to stay on the balls of your feet so you don't get side-stepped.

- ✓ Use quicker and shorter steps in approaching the attacking player and be careful not to plant your feet.

- ✓ Take a boxer's stance, with your hands up and elbows low so as to reinforce your leverage and the force of contact.

- ✓ Use your foot and shoulder on the same side in dipping and stepping into the tackle.

- ✓ Wrap your arms around the attacking player and then pull him while driving from your legs.

- ✓ Put your entire body into the contact to achieve greater power and more force.

- ✓ Allow forward momentum by maintaining leg drive.

Aside from these points, you should also bear in mind that the side-on tackle is much safer to execute, as it involves less confrontation. The risk for injury is therefore lesser, though you'll be applying practically the same techniques and body positions described above.

Another type of tackle is the smother tackle, where you need to be more upright in executing your defence and you attempt to put your arms around the attacking player's arms and the ball.

The objective here is to prevent the attacking player from passing the ball or releasing it so as to score a try.

Again, the same basic techniques, body positions, and steps should apply. Take note, though, that the smother tackle is highly dangerous and therefore isn't recommended for inexperienced players.

Remember as well that tackles above the shoulder line are prohibited and have corresponding penalties.

Lifting and dropping are also prohibited, as it's highly dangerous and may cause some serious injuries.

Always remember that defence is essential for winning a rugby match and the tackle is an integral part of any team's defence strategies. This is why you need to learn and master this skill.

Improving Your Skills

While rugby can be a very rewarding game, it can also be extremely tough and physical. You therefore need to physically and mentally prepare yourself for the rigors of this game.

Remember as well that regardless of your position, there are some core skills you need to constantly work on in order to improve your overall performance in the sport of rugby.

General Fitness

Rugby is such a physical game that you can't really expect to be any good at it without achieving at least the most basic fitness level.

The task of surviving on the playing field for eighty minutes is no mean feat, which is why you need to prepare yourself before the season starts. An effective off-season training necessarily includes going for regular runs.

Your goal in this case is to be able to run for at least five kilometres when the season finally starts.

Aside from this, it's also advisable to engage in other general fitness exercises that get your heart going such as walking, cycling, and swimming.

Varying your fitness training exercises allows you to work different muscles and keeps you motivated.

Ball Skills

Whatever your position is, you need to have some core ball skills to become a good rugby player. While it can be a bit difficult to work on these ball skills on your own, there are always a few skills you can effectively work on regardless of how many training mates you have.

There's a wide range of grid drills you can work on if you have other players to train with. If you don't have training mates, then you may have to use your creativity a bit.

For example, you could kick up and unders to yourself or practice line out throws against the wall. These exercises might make you feel a bit silly at first, but they'll surely offer you some great benefits.

Strength

Needless to say, a strong player has a great advantage in a sport as physical as rugby. This is why it's very important for you to work on your strength.

The best way to do so is through weight training. Of course, the specific exercises you engage in should be the ones that can best benefit you in the position that you play.

Speed

Obviously, it's more important for loose forwards and backs to constantly work on increasing their speed, but you can still benefit from increased speed even when you're playing a different position. The best way to improve your speed is to do sprint drills.

Bear in mind that anyone has the ability to develop muscle memory, so if you keep working on your speed, you will surely be able to improve it over time.

Even when you think you've reached the limits of your speed, there may still be room for improvement, although it may take a bit more time for results to be seen.

Above all, you should remember that the more effort you put into your training, the more results you're likely to get out of your game.

The off-season is the best time to work on improving your skills, so you shouldn't waste any opportunity to do so. You need to get going so you can look forward to a good season ahead.

In-Season Fitness

While the off-season may be the best time to improve your rugby skills, that doesn't mean you should completely neglect training during the season.

In fact, it's important to keep your fitness level up to make sure you perform well in every single match you play.

After all, intense matches can take their toll and may even cause some minor injuries.

Following are some basic principles you may adhere to in order to keep yourself fit in-season.

1. Focus on health and fitness through proper nutrition

By focusing on proper nutrition, your recovery will be effectively enhanced and you'll therefore be able to train with more intensity. Your immunity will also be strengthened and your overall performance will improve.

You should always bear in mind the basic principles of health and nutrition, which includes proper hydration, the inclusion of fruits and vegetables in most of your daily meals, and getting eight to ten hours of sleep each night.

You should also learn to manage your stress levels by engaging in recovery sessions throughout the week.

Take note that protein isn't the end all and be all of athletic nutrition. It's best to eat a well-balanced diet and stick to poultry and fish as protein sources at this time.

2. Beginners need to get to the gym

The game of rugby is changing and physics is now playing a huge role in the sport. So, if you're not already working out at the gym at least twice each week, then you need to start fitting that into your schedule.

It's important for you to increase your strength so as to meet the demands of the game. Two 45-minute sessions of power lifts with low reps, high intensity, and a lot of sets should do the trick. This should effectively improve your recovery and reduce the risk for injury.

3. Focus on recovery

You'll naturally be placing your body under a significant amount of stress during the season.

You therefore need to balance this with plenty of recovery. Some excellent recovery options are Epsom salts bath, massage, sauna, walks, pool recovery, cat-naps, and stretching.

4. Step up every three weeks

Train harder every third week. You could choose to add one more session or perhaps increase the intensity of your exercises. Strongman conditioning for about 30-45 minutes would be ideal for this week. The additional stress will have a rebound effect on the following week.

5. Slow down every four weeks

In contrast to the third week, you need to reduce your training volume every fourth week. You could perhaps take a day or two off and then switch from conditioning sessions to recovery sessions.

On this week, you should also sleep more and take things easy. You need to give your system a chance to recharge. Physically, you'll notice that you're ready to do more and mentally, you'll feel a lot fresher as a result.

Be sure to follow the guidelines outlined above to keep yourself fresh and ready to perform at optimum levels all throughout the rugby season.

Understanding the Referee's Signals

As a rugby player, you need to understand the play that's happening on the field so you can react accordingly.

Subsequently, you also need to understand the signals made by the referee, as they reflect the play that's just occurred.

These signals indicate when a team is awarded a free kick, why penalties are awarded, and why a team is given advantage in play. They're also used for scoring a play.

The referee is also responsible for keeping time and indicating the end of game time. Here are some of the different referee signals and what they mean.

Advantage
A referee indicates a team has advantage by stretching his arm out at waist level and pointing it towards the awarded team. This means play is allowed to continue with the non-offending team on attack instead of being stopped for penalty.

Forward Pass

In this case, the refereed gestures with his hand as if he was making an imaginary forward pass, which is illegal in rugby. The scrum put will then be given to the team that didn't make the mistake.

Free Kick

When awarding a free kick, the referee will raise his arm, bend it at the elbow, and then point towards the team that's awarded a free kick.

High Tackle

This signal indicates that a player has made an illegal high tackle. The referee holds his arm straight across his neck, right under his chin.

Killing the Ball

The referee indicates that a player failed to stay on his feet when joining a ruck. He will point his arm downwards and then move it up and down.

Knock On

To indicate that the ball has been knocked forward, the referee will raise his arm over his head and then move his open hand forwards and backwards. He will then tap both of his palms together.

Obstruction

This signal indicates that a player has made an illegal stop. In this case, the referee crosses his arms across his chest.

Penalty Kick

The referee gives the non-offending team the option to either execute a penalty kick or a scrum by facing the sideline and then pointing towards the non-offending team with his arm straight and in an upward angle.

Slow Release

When the referee feels that a player didn't release the ball immediately after a tackle, he brings both of his hands to his chest as if holding an imaginary ball. A penalty will then be given to the other team at the area where the offence happened.

Try

Standing on the try line, the referee faces the team that scored and then raises his arm over his head as he blows his whistle. The referee's back will be towards the dead ball line.

Knowing how to interpret the referee's signals will increase your understanding and enjoyment of the game of rugby.

While rugby is a highly physical game, it also requires a significant amount of mental alertness, since you'll have to interpret and react to plays very quickly.

By knowing what the referee's signals mean, you can easily plan your next move.

Made in the USA
Lexington, KY
13 November 2013